RUSSELL WILSON

SUPERSTAR QUARTERBACK

BY TED COLEMAN

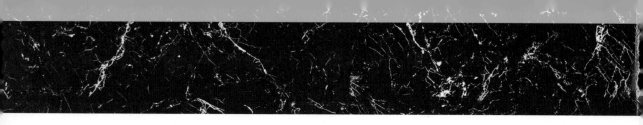

Book design by Jake Nordby
Cover design by Jake Slavik

Photographs ©: Ted S. Warren/AP Images, cover, 1; Jeff Roberson/AP Images, 4; Chris O'Meara/AP Images, 7; Nick Wass/AP Images, 8; Brian Westerholt/Four Seam Images/AP Images, 10; John Green/Cal Sport Media/AP Images, 13; Stephen Brashear/AP Images, 14; Brian Garfinkel/AP Images, 17; Paul Spinelli/AP Images, 19; Steve Dykes/Getty Images Sport/Getty Images, 20; Shutterstock Images, 21 (top), 25, 30; Kevin Terrell/AP Images, 21 (bottom); Mike Roemer/AP Images, 22; Julio Cortez/AP Images, 27; Red Line Editorial, 29

Press Box Books, an imprint of Press Room Editions.

Library of Congress Control Number: 2020901593

ISBN
978-1-63494-215-7 (library bound)
978-1-63494-233-1 (paperback)
978-1-63494-251-5 (epub)
978-1-63494-269-0 (hosted ebook)

Distributed by North Star Editions, Inc.
2297 Waters Drive
Mendota Heights, MN 55120
www.northstareditions.com

Printed in the United States of America
082020

About the Author

Ted Coleman is a sportswriter who lives in Louisville, Kentucky.

TABLE OF CONTENTS

1 SUPER BOWL CHAMP

Russell Wilson barely had time to soak in the atmosphere of his first Super Bowl. Just 12 seconds into the game on February 2, 2014, his Seattle Seahawks teammates on defense gave him a lead. A bad snap by the Denver Broncos sailed into the end zone for a safety. Seattle led 2-0 before Wilson even took the field.

The Broncos had a future Hall of Fame quarterback in Peyton Manning. But it was Wilson who looked like the old pro. While Manning struggled to make an impact,

Russell Wilson throws a pass in the Super Bowl on February 2, 2014.

Seattle's second-year quarterback excelled. He used his legs and his strong throwing arm to keep the Seahawks offense moving. He threw two touchdown passes in the game. It was what fans had come to expect from Wilson.

But it was what Wilson did not do that helped the Seahawks dominate Denver. He didn't fumble, and he didn't throw an interception. Manning threw two interceptions and lost one fumble.

Wilson was calm and steady for Seattle. On his first touchdown pass, he got the ball to one of his best playmakers and let him go to work. Wilson hit Jermaine Kearse with a quick pass

Wilson holds the Lombardi Trophy after the Seahawks beat the Broncos.

five yards downfield. Then Kearse weaved his way through the defense for a 23-yard score. It put the game away.

Seattle won 43–8. Wilson led a true team effort. People once thought he was too short to be an NFL quarterback. The Super Bowl trophy he held proved them wrong.

2 THE BALLPLAYER

Russell Wilson was always a leader. In elementary school, he sometimes led the other kids in activities when the teacher left the room. That leadership translated to sports. Russell played baseball, basketball, and football growing up.

Russell was born on November 29, 1988. He grew up in Richmond, Virginia. He loved playing sports with his dad and older brother. Russell's dad played both football and baseball at Dartmouth

Russell began his college football career at North Carolina State.

Russell also played baseball in college.

College and participated in one NFL training camp. Baseball and football grew to be Russell's favorites as well.

Football became Russell's main sport in high school. As a senior, he threw for

3,009 yards and ran for 1,132 yards. He led his team to the state championship. Colleges could see Russell was a great athlete. But they worried he was too short to be a great quarterback. Russell received scholarship offers from only a couple of colleges. He accepted one from North Carolina State.

No quarterback emerged as a clear starter for the Wolfpack to start the 2008 season. Russell won the job with his steady play. At one point, he threw 249 passes in a row without an interception. He was picked off just once all year. Wilson was one of the best quarterbacks

BASEBALL CAREER

Russell did play two years of minor league baseball with the Rockies organization. A second baseman, he hit .229 with 26 runs batted in at the Class-A level in 2010 and 2011. The Texas Rangers acquired him in 2013, and he was traded to the New York Yankees in 2018. Russell never played in the minors for either team. But he did participate in spring training four times.

in the conference the next two years. In 2010 he finished runner-up for conference player of the year.

Meanwhile, Russell also played baseball. The Colorado Rockies selected him in the fourth round of the 2010 Major League Baseball Draft. Russell played minor league baseball that summer. He planned to attend Rockies spring training in 2011. But his football coaches were worried Russell wasn't committed to football. Russell said later his coach told him he would not start for the Wolfpack in 2011.

Russell had one year left of college football to play. He decided to transfer and play somewhere else. He chose the University of Wisconsin. Russell had his best season yet and one of the best in Wisconsin history. He threw a school-record 33 touchdown passes and just

Russell scores a touchdown against Oregon in the Rose Bowl.

four interceptions while leading the Badgers to the Rose Bowl.

Russell got better and better in college. He finished his career playing for a big program in a huge bowl game. The National Football League (NFL) was his next stop.

3 SAVING SEATTLE

The Seahawks chose Wilson with the 75th pick in the 2012 draft. The pick was criticized heavily in Seattle. The Seahawks had just given a big contract to free agent quarterback Matt Flynn. Plus Wilson was short. It wasn't clear what the team planned to do with him.

Wilson had his own plan. It was to win the starting job. And that was exactly what he did. Wilson outplayed Flynn in the preseason. Head coach Pete Carroll

As a rookie, Wilson impressed Seahawks head coach Pete Carroll in training camp.

named him the Week 1 starter before the preseason even ended.

The choice was a surprise to many. But Carroll was proven right. Wilson gave fans a memorable moment at home in Week 3 against Green Bay. He threw a Hail Mary touchdown pass as time expired to beat Green Bay. The 2012 season turned into a wild ride for fans. Wilson got better as the year went on. He threw 26 touchdown passes, which tied an NFL rookie record. And he helped the Seahawks earn a spot in the postseason.

In his first career playoff game, Wilson and the Seahawks fell behind. They trailed Washington 14-0 after one quarter. But Wilson led a comeback. He and the offense scored 24 straight points. And the Seattle defense tightened up to not allow another point.

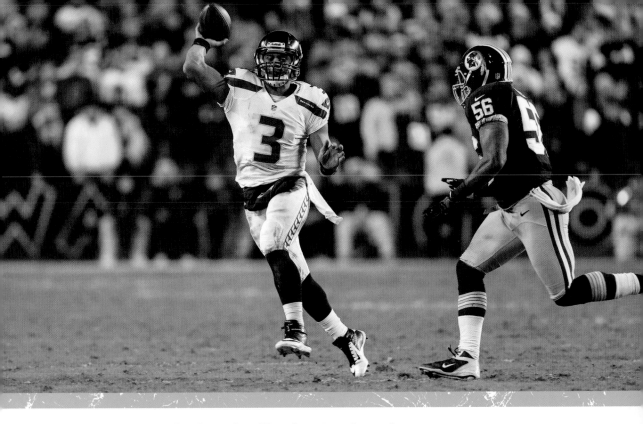

Wilson helped rally the Seahawks past Washington in his first playoff game.

The Seahawks lost in the next round, but they were building a great team.

Seattle had Super Bowl hopes in 2013. Wilson was even better, and so was the defense. The result was a 13–3 record and a blowout win over the Denver Broncos in the Super Bowl.

Wilson set new career highs in passing and rushing yards in 2014. Seattle returned to the playoffs. Repeating as Super Bowl champs looked like a long shot in the conference championship game. Wilson had more interceptions than completions in the first half against Green Bay. Seattle trailed 19–7 with just four minutes left.

CHARITY WORK

Wilson started the Why Not You Foundation in 2014. The name is meant to inspire kids to pursue their dreams. Wilson credited his father with instilling the "why not you?" mentality in him. The foundation funds initiatives to help children. Wilson also volunteers his time to help children who are suffering.

Wilson then led an amazing comeback. First he marched the offense 69 yards in seven plays. Wilson scored from the 1. Then Seattle recovered an onside kick. Four plays later, the Seahawks were back in the end zone on a 24-yard run by Marshawn

Wilson and running back Marshawn Lynch helped fuel Seattle's comeback against Green Bay.

Lynch. Green Bay managed to send the game to overtime, but Wilson won it with a 35-yard touchdown pass.

The New England Patriots turned the table on the Seahawks in the Super Bowl. Wilson's last-second pass from the Patriots 1-yard line was intercepted. New England won 28–24.

PITCH AND CATCH

Everyone knows Russell Wilson can throw. In a 2016 game against the Philadelphia Eagles, he showed that he can catch, too, when he hauled in a touchdown pass from wide receiver Doug Baldwin on a trick play.

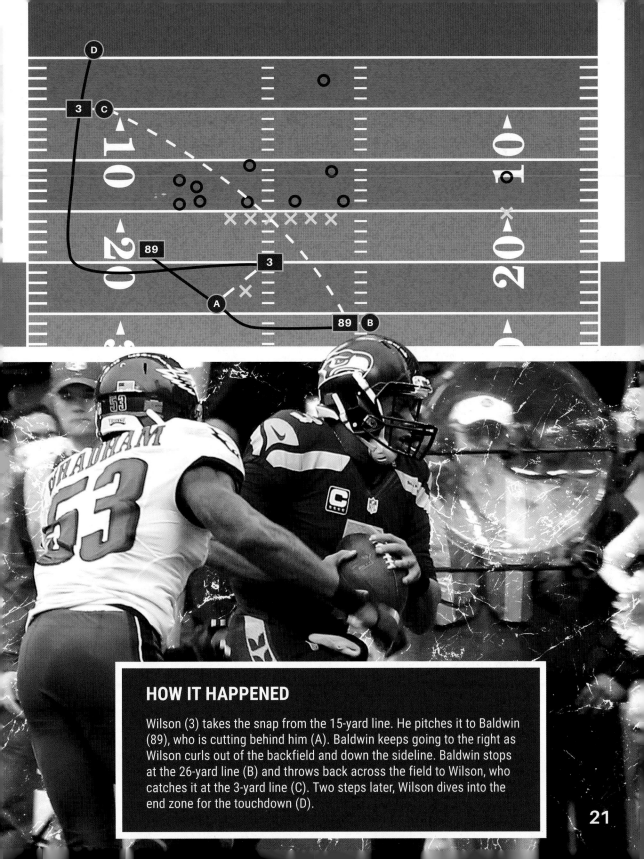

HOW IT HAPPENED

Wilson (3) takes the snap from the 15-yard line. He pitches it to Baldwin (89), who is cutting behind him (A). Baldwin keeps going to the right as Wilson curls out of the backfield and down the sideline. Baldwin stops at the 26-yard line (B) and throws back across the field to Wilson, who catches it at the 3-yard line (C). Two steps later, Wilson dives into the end zone for the touchdown (D).

4 FRANCHISE QUARTERBACK

The 2015 season turned out to be Wilson's best yet. He posted career highs with 4,024 passing yards and 34 touchdown passes. Both of those were new team records. But Seattle's defense was starting to decline. Some players were slowed by age, and some left for other teams.

Seattle's record slipped to 10-6 in 2015. Then it was 10-5-1 in 2016, and 9-7 in 2017. Wilson continued to play well. He fought through some injuries in 2016.

Wilson is known as one of the NFL's most accurate passers.

But he played through the pain and made all 16 starts. And he led the Seahawks to the playoffs for the fifth straight year. He won his eighth playoff game in the 2016 season, the most for any NFL quarterback in his first five years.

The playoff streak was snapped the next year even though Wilson was healthy and had a strong season. He led the NFL with 34 touchdown passes. The Seahawks went 9–7, but they missed the playoffs by one game.

Things didn't look much better for 2018. Big stars on offense and defense left the team before the season. But Seattle bounced back with a strong season. Wilson set a new career high with

FAMOUS COUPLE

Wilson started dating Grammy Award–winning singer Ciara in 2015. They got married in 2016 and had a daughter in 2017. Wilson and Ciara are both active in running Wilson's charity, the Why Not You Foundation.

Wilson and Ciara walk the red carpet at the 2015 Kids' Choice Sports Awards.

35 touchdown passes. And the Seahawks were back in the playoffs.

Seattle extended its commitment to Wilson before 2019. A new contract made him the highest-paid player in the league. Seattle expected Wilson to keep winning big games.

Wilson nearly clinched the top seed in the 2019 playoffs for Seattle in the last game of the season against San Francisco. With time running out and Seattle trailing by five, Wilson completed a short pass inside the 5-yard line. But the receiver was stopped just inches from the goal line, and Seattle lost.

The Seahawks still made the playoffs. But they had to go on the road to Philadelphia. Wilson beat the Eagles almost by himself. He passed for 325 yards and rushed for 45 more. Seattle won 17–9.

That set up a game with Green Bay in the next round. Wilson had been successful against the Packers in the past. Down 21–3 at the half, Wilson again tried to rally the

The Eagles had no answer for Wilson in the 2019 playoffs.

Seahawks. But the comeback fell short, and they lost 28–23.

Wilson was showing no signs of slowing down. But the Super Bowl title was starting to feel like a long time ago. Seahawks fans hoped their franchise quarterback had another championship run in him.

TIMELINE

1. **Cincinnati, Ohio (November 29, 1988)**
   Russell Wilson is born.

2. **Richmond, Virginia (2007)**
   Wilson graduates from Collegiate School in his hometown of Richmond.

3. **Raleigh, North Carolina (September 20, 2008)**
   Wilson wins his first college game while playing for the North Carolina State Wolfpack.

4. **Pasadena, California (January 2, 2012)**
   After transferring to Wisconsin, Wilson leads the Badgers to the Rose Bowl.

5. **New York, New York (April 27, 2012)**
   Wilson is chosen 75th overall by the Seattle Seahawks in the NFL Draft.

6. **East Rutherford, New Jersey (February 2, 2014)**
   Wilson and the Seahawks win the first Super Bowl in franchise history over the Denver Broncos.

7. **Glendale, Arizona (February 1, 2015)**
   Wilson's last pass of the Super Bowl is intercepted as the Seahawks fall short in their bid for a repeat.

8. **Philadelphia, Pennsylvania (January 5, 2020)**
   Wilson accounts for 370 yards of total offense and wins his ninth playoff game 17-9 over the Eagles.

AT-A-GLANCE

Birth date: November 29, 1988

Birthplace: Cincinnati, Ohio

Position: Quarterback

Throws: Right

Height: 5 feet 11 inches

Weight: 215 pounds

Current team: Seattle Seahawks (2012–)

Past teams: North Carolina State Wolfpack (2008-10), Wisconsin Badgers (2011)

Major awards: Super Bowl champion (2013), Pro Bowl (2012-13, 2015, 2017-19)

Accurate through the 2019 NFL season and playoffs.

GLOSSARY

conference
A group of teams that compete against each other in sports.

draft
A system that allows teams to acquire new players coming into a league.

franchise quarterback
A quarterback capable of leading a team for a number of years.

Hail Mary
A long pass to the end zone at the end of a half or a game.

onside kick
A kickoff that is purposely short with the hope that the kicking team can recover the ball.

playmakers
Talented players who often make game-changing plays.

preseason
A period of practice before the regular season with games that do not count in the standings.

rookie
A first-year player.

scholarship
Money awarded to a student to pay for education expenses.

transfer
To move to a different school.

Books

Doeden, Matt. *The Super Bowl: Chasing Football Immortality*. Minneapolis, MN: Millbrook Press, 2018.

Ryan, Todd. *Seattle Seahawks*. Minneapolis, MN: Abdo Publishing, 2020.

Whiting, Jim. *The Story of the Seattle Seahawks*. Mankato, MN: Creative Education, 2019.

Websites

Russell Wilson College Stats
www.sports-reference.com/cfb/players/russell-wilson-1.html

Russell Wilson Pro Stats
www.pro-football-reference.com/players/W/WilsRu00.htm

Seattle Seahawks
www.seahawks.com

INDEX